MUSIC MAGIC

How Parents Can Help Their Children Love Music

MUSIC MAGIC

How Parents Can Help Their Children Love Music

By Carmen De Angelis

Published by
Bookstand Publishing
Morgan Hill, CA 95037
3679_3

Copyright © 2012 by Carmen De Angelis
All rights reserved. No part of this publication may be reproduced or transmitted in any form or by any means, electronic or mechanical, including photocopy, recording, or any information storage and retrieval system, without permission in writing from the copyright owner.

978-1-61863-312-5

Printed in the United States of America

www.bookstandpublishing.com

PREFACE

This parents music guide has been designed to help parents better understand the value of music as an important part of the learning process.

As a depression baby, music was the last thing on the minds of a house full of jobless adults. The one bright light in our home was a player piano. My sister enrolled me in a piano course at Hull House in Chicago, Illinois, the first depressed area social center in the United States. Benny Goodman was also enrolled in the same center.

However, when I tried to practice my mother would say, "stop making all that noise". Two lessons at Hull House and my mothers' telling me to stop making noise found me out playing with my friends. Music at school consisted of singing one song a week.

Parent encouragement is a serious part of the total learning process.
Kind words, a set practice schedule, and a quiet place to practice are all part of the active thing we call parental encouragement.

ACKNOWLEDGEMENTS

My wife Pat and our family

Kali, for her work on the cover
and the pictures

Gavin for picture with French Horn

Ashlee for cover picture with violin

Youth Outreach Directors

and Mindy for Editing.

GETTING TO KNOW YOU

This is your music guide book. We want to help you help your child/children grow in their best possible light. If you have questions, comments, suggestions, some subject you like and want more of, let us know.

You can contact us at:

Email: wdhnow@cfl.rr.com

Contact Amazon to buy more books.

Thanks to Book Stand Publishing Company for all their help.

INTRODUCTION

Before the advent of formal education, it was the responsibility of the parents to educate their children. As we became more sophisticated and entered the industrial revolution the responsibility still remained with the parents but was relegated to more formal professionals called school systems.

The building of a curriculum was left to the professionals whether a one room school or a city district system. As parents pulled away from the decision making, regarding what subjects were to be taught, the arts became a minor issue.

We have come full circle. The responsibility to provide for the academic pursuit of the arts has come back to parents.

This guide will;

- Give parents some starting points at which to begin an effective music program regardless of the child's age.

- Present research which supports the importance of   music in the development of a child's learning process.
- Provide references for further study.

Music can be a magical step toward building a strong positive character and strength in a child.

The magic of music is addressed in each section of this book. The words written in these pages, however, are not the magic. The magic comes as a result of the effort a student exerts in the pursuit of excellence through learning the selected music craft.

START AT THE BEGINNING

Where is the beginning? That place is whatever age your child is right now.

Women who have had children know that a great deal of bonding goes on during the pregnancy period. Certainly, there is bonding between the mother and the child, husband and wife, and other children in the family. However, another area of bonding could be between the mother and the baby through music. Exposing the baby to music while in the womb will do its share of bonding and begin a whole rhythm cycle. Much research has been done on this subject. (The topic of music and the unborn child is being addressed by this author in a text in progress. See the Reference Section, author Abrams, R M (1995).

Any time between pregnancy and the high school years is a good time to get started.

TABLE OF CONTENTS

1. Why Music? — 1
2. 13 Questions Parents Should Ask Before Beginning A Music Program — 7
3. The Advantages of Music Training On Child Development — 11
4. Know What Music is Available in Your Community — 13
5. Music Around The World — 19
6. First Exposures to Music — 23
7. Songs for Children — 27
8. Time to Get Started — 31
9. Internet References — 33
10. Research References — 39

Bibliography — 45

Chapter 1

WHY MUSIC?

<u>Music lessons help develop thinking skills.</u>

Young children who received a year of musical training showed brain changes and superior memory compared with children who did not receive the instruction. FUJIOKA, T., ROSS, B., KAKIGI, R., PANTEV, C. AND TRAINORK L, BRAIN, A JOURNAL OF NEUROLOGY, OXFORD UNIVERSITY PRESS, SEPT. 2006.
Another study examined the influence of music education on nonmusical abilities. They looked for the effect of music lessons on academic performance and cognitive abilities. The study showed that students who participate in music lessons showed statistically higher intelligence quotations than students who did not take music lessons. GLENN SCHELLENBERG, MUSIC LESSONS ENHANCE IQ, PSYCHOLOGICAL SCIENCE, VOL. 15, NO. 8, 2004.
<u>Playing music builds motivation and self-esteem.</u>

A Columbia University study showed that students in the arts are found to be more cooperative with teachers and peers, more self-confident and better able to express themselves. BURTON, J., HOROWITZ. R., ABELES, H., CHAMPIONS OF CHANGE, ARTS EDUCATION PARTNERSHIP, 1999.

Learning music builds skills for the future.

The skills gained through sequential music instruction, including discipline and the ability to analyze and solve problems, communicate and work cooperatively, are vital for success in the 21st century.
U S HOUSE OF REPRESENTATIVES, CONCURRENT RESOLUTION 355, MARCH 6, 2006.

The advantages of the arts.

The advantages derived from music education can be divided into four parts, which are:

1. Advantages gained by the community

2. Advantages developed through school

3. Advantages obtained by student broadening his/her intelligence.

4. Advantages by providing the students of music with positive choices to consider when faced with negative choices in their environment.

I. The advantages which are gained by the community.

Music is a part of the fabric of our society. It is everywhere in our culture.
Music is present in our church, school, social gatherings, sports activities, television and movies.

The U.S. Department of Education lists the arts as subjects that college-bound middle and junior high school students should take. stating, "any potential college should participate in the arts and music as a valuable experience that broadens students understanding and appreciation of the world around them...GETTING READY FOR COLLEGE EARLY: A HANDBOOK FOR PARENTS OF STUDENTS IN THE MIDDLE AND JUNIOR HIGH SCHOOL YEARS, U.S. DEPARTMENT OF EDUCATION, 1997

The arts create jobs, increase the local tax base, boost tourism, spur growth in related businesses (hotels, restaurants, printing, etc.) and improve the overall quality of life for our cities and towns. On a national level, nonprofit art institutions and organizations generate an estimated $37 billion in economic activity and returns $3.4 billion in federal income taxes to the U.S. Treasury each year. AMERICAN ARTS ALLIANCE FACT SHEET, OCTOBER 1989

II. Advantages developed through school

A study of 237 second grade children uses piano keyboard training and newly designed math software to demonstrate improvement in math skills. The group scored 27% higher on proportional math and fractions tests than children that used only the math software. GRAZIONO, AMY, MATTHEW PETERSON,

AND GORDON SHAW, "ENHANCED LEARNING OF PROPORTIONAL MATH THROUGH MUSIC TRAINING AND SPATIAL-TEMPORAL TRAINING." NEUROLOGICAL RESEARCH 21 (MARCH 1999).

Students with coursework/experience in music performance and music appreciation scored higher on the SAT. Students in music performance scored 57 points higher on the verbal and 41 points higher on the math, and students in music appreciation scored 63 points higher on verbal and 44 points higher on the math, than did students with no arts participation. COLLEGE-BOUND SENIORS NATIONAL REPORT: PROFILE OF SAT PROGRAM TEST TAKERS, PRINCETON, NJ. THE COLLEGE ENTRANCE EXAMINATION BOARD, 2001.

III. Advantages in students strengthening their intelligence capabilities

A research team exploring the link between music and intelligence reported that music training is far superior to computer instruction in dramatically enhancing children's abstract reasoning skills, the skills necessary for learning math and sciences. SHAW, RAUSCHER, LEVINE, WRIGHT, DENNIS AND NEWCOMB, "MUSIC TRAINING CAUSES LONG-TERM ENHANCEMENT OF PRESCHOOL CHILDREN'S SPATIAL-

TEMPORAL REASONING," NEUROLOGICAL RESEARCH, VOL. 19, FEBRUARY 1997.

In the Kindergarten classes of the school district of Kettle Moraine, Wisconsin, children who were given music instruction scored 48 percent higher on spatial-temporal skill tests than those who did not receive music training. RAUSCHER, F.H., AND UPAN, M.A. (1999). CLASSROOM KEYBOARD INSTRUCTION IN PRESS, EARLY CHILDHOOD RESEARCH QUARTERLY.

IV. Providing music students with positive choices to consider when faced with negative choices in their environment.

Studying music encourages self-discipline and diligence, traits that carry over into intellectual pursuits and lead to effective study and work habits. Creating and performing music promotes self-expression and provides self-gratification while giving pleasure to others.

For these reasons, and more, music deserves strong support in our educational systems. MICHAEL E. DEEBAKEY, M.D., LEADING HEART SURGEON, BAYLOR COLLEGE OF MUSIC.

Music education opens doors that help children pass from school into the world around them. It is a world of work, culture and hidden pit falls. It is here that our young people must have positive choices ready to replace the negative choices which they will meet in life. GERALD FORD, FORMER PRESIDENT OF THE UNITED STATES OF AMERICA.

How does a parent know where to start?

Pre-school is the perfect time to introduce children to the art of learning and taking part in music In preparing your child/children to take part in a music program, critical questions should be asked. Chapter two will guide you in preparing a comprehensive set of questions which will get you pointed in the right direction.

Chapter 2

13 Questions Parents Should Ask Before Beginning a Music Program.

1. How old should my child be before beginning a music program?

A. The answer depends on your personal situation. If, for example, yours is a musically oriented family, and one or both parents play an instrument, the time to start may be at a very early age. Generally, 3 years of age to begin formal training with an instrument seems to be the consensus of opinion among music teachers and our research.

2. Who should decide what instrument he/she should play?

A. Music teachers at some of our local elementary schools have started students in rhythmic moving and singing at the preschool and kindergarten level (4 to 6 years old). The students then progress to the recorder and move up to wind instruments by seven to eight years of age. Next move, depending on the child and their choice, could be to piano, violin and/or bell chorus if available.

Depending on the individual child's choice, piano and violin seem to be the instruments recommended from age 3 – 5. Beyond 5 years it's the child's choice with financial considerations playing an obvious part.

3. What type of a music program does your school have?

A. The answer to this question will have a lot to do with if your child is attending a public, private, or home school. If public or private, make an appointment with the school music teacher. (If your school does not have music teacher talk to the principal.) If your school does not have a music program, kindly remind the principal that, according to the "No Child Left Behind Act," music is part of the Core Curriculum and should be included in their program.

When you have your meeting with the music teacher listen for names like, Orff, Dolcroze, Kadely, and Susuki. If she/he is using any one of these somewhere in the music program they are headed in the right direction. (More on these programs, Orff, etc. will be addressed in the chapter entitled Music Around the World.)

4. Do any of your children's friends play an instrument?

A. The parents of your child's friend may share some insights in choosing an instrument.

5. Does your child comment on any particular instrument.

A. The comments could show interest.

6. Do you play an instrument?

A. Seeing you practice might make an impression on your child.

7. If your school has a music program is it a part of the school day or is it an after school program?

  A. The answer may make a difference in your daily family schedule.

8. Are private lessons available?

  A. Feasibility depends on your finances and time schedule.

9. Does your school have a band?

A. Whether your school has a band or not, it is also a good idea to get familiar with the community and find out what other music opportunities are available. This guide has a chapter devoted to "Know What Music is Available in Your Community".   Most areas have bands, orchestras and some have children's beginning bands. Check with your chamber of commerce.

10. How many days a week does the school music class meet for instruction?

11. Is there a calendar of events announcing when the performances are held? There is usually a school newsletter which gives event performances.

12. Are there music instruments available or must they be purchased? Is there a rental program? Is there a lease program with an option to buy?

13. How do I know my child is ready to begin learning to play an instrument?

A. If your child wants to play any instrument at any age a safe positive response might be,
"That's great, let's talk to a music teacher about that and see if she/he thinks you're ready."
Some areas have nonprofit organizations that provide free summer workshops for children who want to learn how to play a musical instrument.

(The PAL – Police Athletic League program of Melbourne has, in the past, provided such a program.) Check with your local chamber of commerce to see if your community has a similar program.

Perhaps the most important question which should be asked is; what advantages are derived from the study of music in the development of a child's learning process?

Chapter 3

The Advantages of Music Training on Child Development

The formative years are a time of exploration and discovery. We, as parents, should continuously search for ways to share new avenues of discovery to help our children strengthen the basic skills involved in learning. Self-esteem, coordination, the ability to focus and develop patience in practicing, are basic needs essential to a well rounded child development program.

Building Self-Esteem Children need a constant barrage of positive reinforcement if they are to develop the strong self-esteem characteristic necessary to meet the challenges of their growing up years. There is no faster way to acquire a positive character than to become part of a music program. Success in learning to play a music instrument or being part of a chorus creates a winning atmosphere with every performance. The encouragement of a teacher, the applause of the audience, the enthusiasm of parents and friends, all serve to feed the building blocks of a success oriented character.

Coordination Physical and mental dexterity are abilities essential in sports, computer and machine operations, knitting, etc. Practicing a musical instrument, likewise, requires dexterity in the same skills.

Another element of coordination is the social aspect of developing the ability to work with others as a team. The contribution of individual talents to form a united whole is the basis upon which team activities are founded. Team work is also important part of being part of a band, orchestra or chorus.

Focus Learning to play an instrument of any kind requires serious attention the ability to focus. The time required to practice playing a music instrument is a transferable task attention exercise. Attention to detail is the important lesson learned, whether it's a music instrument, studying history or baking a cake.

Patience When choosing between playing an instrument and not playing, there is a clear advantage in the area of developing patience. Patience is the ability to persevere when meeting a challenge. There are many challenges in the study of music, for example; developing a consistent work study habits, learning to follow the conductor's direction and timing of a students instrument performance within the group, are just a few samples of the need for developing student patience. Overcoming each challenge is a step closer to realizing an individuals self worth.

Chapter 4

Know What is Available in Your Community

. We will examine three traditional community organizations in light of their music offerings; schools, churches and nonprofit music organizations.

Schools The simplest and most obvious place to begin is your county neighborhood elementary public school. However, be prepared to accept the fact that your particular elementary school may not provide a music program. Some county school systems have what is called The County Demonstration School. Brevard County Florida has such a program. Demonstration schools focus on a specific discipline, such as math, science or music. Pupils wishing to attend one of these schools must qualify.

There are other avenues to explore in regard to schools. There are private virtual reality academies, private church run schools and private non-denomination schools.
Most of these schools can be reached by internet, yellow pages or your local library. Home school and telephone schools (telephone schools may have different names in each district.) are also available. For information about these call your public school community services department. However, schools are not the only means of becoming part of the music picture.

Churches Your church may have a children's band, or, with enough member interest, be willing to start one. Check your churches weekly bulletin or website for details.

Community Orchestras and Bands Most communities have a local orchestra and or band. Some also have a community youth program, check with your chamber of commerce. You may inquire with the community orchestra director for listings of the teachers of specific instruments. Be sure that they are trained in teaching music. They should havethe least, a college degree in music.

The following is a list of some of the music organizations in Brevard County, Florida. Other communities usually have like organizations. Your local chamber of commerce, library, yellow pages or internet may be of help locating them.

Brevard Chorale: chorale is in partnership with Brevard Community College. For more information call (321) 433 7385 or visit www.brevardchorale.org

Brevard Community Chorus and Orchestra: with approximately 100 plus voices present concerts with music by Beethoven, Handel and Mozart. For more information call (321) 433-7385.

Brevard Symphony Orchestra: is in cooperation with the Brevard School Board, children orchestra. Positions are available by audition. For more information call
(321) 242-2024, e-mail bso@ju.net, web site www.brevardsymphony.com.

Community Band of Brevard: their purpose is to educate members and keep band music alive. Auditions not required. For more information e-mail mike@communitybandofbrevard.org

Harbor City Harmonizers: purpose is to sing acappella and perform in four part Harmony in the Barbershop Style. The chorus presents Christmas and spring shows and will sing by request. Valentine serenades available by Quartets who also sing for special occasions. For more information call (321) 213 – 9424 or - www.hcharmonizers.com

Indialantic Chamber Singers : is a small, professional – quality group of volunteer musicians.

Melbourne Chamber Music Society: provides the community with five world class guest groups each year to perform at St. Marks United Methodist church, 2030 N. SR A1A, Indialantic. For more information call (321) 751-4998 or (321) 2785 or visit www. melbournechambermusicsociety.com

Melbourne Community Orchestra: is composed of retired professionals and advanced amateurs of all ages. For more information call (321) 952-9952.

The Melbourne Municipal Band: made up of 100 professionals and amateurs, they perform free concerts and have assembled a Dixieland Band, Youth Band and a Swing Band specializing in 40's music dances. For more information call (321) 724-0555.

Platinum Coast Chorus: the women's chorus offers music education and vocal training and performs an annual show once a year. The group is a local chapter of the Sweet Adeline's International. For more information Google - Sweet Adeline's, Melbourne, Florida.

Rock the Silence: brings Christian music to hearing and hearing impaired audiences. The organization also teacher's sign language classes through Brevard County teachers. For more information call (321) 446-1802 or go to the web site, www.rockthesilence.homestead.com

Space Coast Flute Orchestra: features, approximately 42 musicians who play a wide selection of flutes, from piccolo to standard C flute. This orchestra performs concerts throughout Brevard County, Florida. For information call (321) 723 – 7145 or (321) 757-3931

Space Coast Jazz Society: meets in the afternoon, second Sunday monthly for live jazz performances at

the Cocoa Beach Country Club. For more information call (321)
632- 4420 or (321) 453- 4191 Web site, spacecoastjazzsociety.com

Space Coast Pops: provides concerts for the community and sponsors a Brevard Young performing Artists Competition. For more information call (321) 632-7445
Or visit www.spacecoastpops.com

Space Coast Symphony Orchestra: the orchestra was formed to provide mentoring and performance opportunities for young student musicians. For more information call (321) 536-8580 or visit www.spacecoastsymphony.org

The above music organizations are a small sample of what is available in Brevard County. Each area has local offerings.

As the world continues to shrink, the various cultures take from each other those elements of music which their people embrace. Our music has been and continues to be influenced by music from around the world. Four teaching methods found in Chapter 5 have made a mark and continue to grow in this country.

Chapter 5

Music Around the World and How it Affects us

Music is an international language. Some teachers and developers of music curriculum in the U.S. have begun to recognize the international influences guiding music in various parts of the world. Although the introduction of music has a strong influence on the learning process, its' influence on our educational system is slow. Although acceptance of music as a force in the learning process is slow, there is some evidence of its being recognized. There is some movement toward acknowledgement of the research which supports music as a viable influence in the learning process throughout the world.

Four international music teaching methods have been introduced to the United States and have met with some success; The Dalcroze Method, Kodaly method, Orff Schulwerk and Zuzuki Violin program. Parents should be aware of these programs. More information is available through the internet.

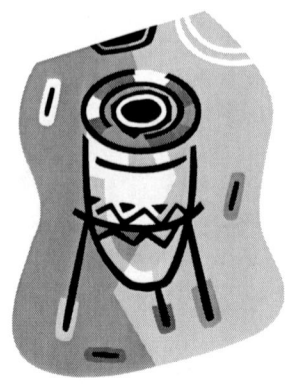

FROM SWITZERLAND

The Dalcroze Method: was developed by Emile Joque – Dalcroze, a Swiss musician and educator. The method is divided into two parts; 1) the use of solfege that is – the learning of essentials of music; theory, tonality, tempo, rhythm, etc. 2) improvisation and eurhythmics – rhythm and jimnastics combined, and improvisation, movements to music with no preparation, done on the spur of the moment.

FROM HUNGARY

Zoltan Kodaly was born in Hungary in 1882 and became a prominent music educator and composer. His trademark was the use of hand signs, music short hand notation and rhythm verbalization. Most American music teachers prefer to use the Hungarian folk music rather than American.

FROM GERMANY

The Orff music program, originated in Germany, is internationally conducted and many communities in our country have the program in place. Hopefully, your community has a program in which you may participate.

The Orff music program in our area, Melbourne, Florida, is being offered at some of the public schools starting at the pre-school level. The program progresses through the middle school. The Orff concept begins with rhythm and progresses to percussion instruments. The children learn timing, movement, improvisation and more.

You would do well to go to your computer and search for your local Orff Music Association. If you are lucky enough to have a program in progress, be sure to visit when they are working with the children.

Carl Orff was a composer and music educator. He created the Off Schulwerk as a special approach to the teaching of music education for the young children of Preschool age. Orff considered the whole body a percussive instrument and students are led to develop their music abilities in a way that parallels the development of western music. His program encourages improvisation and does not believe in adult pressure. Orff developed a special group of instruments including specially designed glockenspiels, xylophones, met allophones, and drums.

FROM JAPAN

Shinichi Suzuki developed his method shortly after World War II and uses music to educate and enhance the lives of its students. The methods basic philosophy is the same as that used in teaching a child his native language. Music basics are taught along with language basics. All the same needs are met; discipline, strong work ethics, a set time table for practice, all becomes part of the child's daily routine.

These are a few of the foreign influences which have helped shape our music learning process. Most methods declare findings in research which profess some success in music helping to positively improve the learning process. (See our chapter on research results.

Chapter 6

First Exposures to Music Remembered

Don Campbell states, in his book <u>The Mozart Effect for Children,</u> traditionally, music has long been a part of childbirth. From ritual dances and songs prescribed in Nigeria to the belly dances of the Middle East, movements originally intended to assist women in bringing a child into the world."

But where does the realization of music and dance all begin?
For the Nigerian baby it is in the ritualistic songs and dance of birth.

As a youth, where did you receive your first exposure to music? Being a depression baby, food on the table was a major need in my family. Music was the last thing on the minds of Italian emigrants in the early 30s.

We did have, however, two musical instruments, a player piano and a radio. My radio was a homework buddy. Every night I would sit at a dinning room table and do my homework. The radio was allowed. One of the best parts of the evening was hearing "the thundering hoof beats of the great horse Silver." Yes, it was The Loan Ranger having another adventure. The music stirred me beyond my homework. Little did I know that I was being exposed to one of the world greatest classics, "The William Tell Overture".

Yes, my first exposure to classical music was not hearing a concert production, but rather, hearing background music to a children's radio program. And there was more.

Children's movie chapters, Buck Rogers, The Green Hornet and so many more.

As I grew older other pieces fell into place. Peter and the wolf, Walt Disney's Fantasia and other movie background music. John Philip Susa's march music certainly played a major part of high school and college band music.

The major recollections are of the songs of the early years. (See Song for Children listed in this guide.)

What are your first remembrances? Your children will have a store of remembrances. Much of their favorites will come from their friends and the music that comes from their generation. There is not much we can control from that prospective. All we can do is try to influence our children at their early ages and hope for the best.

<u>Early childhood programs which may help form a positive music base.</u>

MUSIC TOGETHER –<u>Center for Music and Young Children</u> In this program children are encouraged to hear, think and move freely while they sing. Registration is from birth to five years old. (ph.) 800-728-2692

ORFF SCHULWERK – For children from prenatal to 4 years old. Parent attendance sometimes required.
(Ph.) 216-543-5366

SUZUKI – Child plays scaled down instruments and is taught familiarization of music basics learning to read music notes often experiencing the music making process.

Other Associations and Foundations.

American Association of Kodaly Educators
(Ph.) 701-235-0366

Foundation for Music – Basic Learning
Greensboro, NC

Kindermusik International, Greensboro, NC
(Ph.) 800-628-5687

Musikgarten, Greensboro, NC 800-216-6864

Chapter 7

Songs For Children

At Pregnancy
Rocka Bye Baby
Twinkle Twinkle, Little Star
You Are My Sunshine
Star Light Star Bright
This Little Light of Mine

At Infancy
It's Raining, It's Pouring
Lullaby and Good Night
Baa, Baa Black Sheep
Kumbaya
Mary Had a Little Lamb

For Babies
Pat-a-Cake
I'm a Little Teapot
Jack and Jill
Ride a Cock Horse
This Little Piggy Went to Market

For Toddlers
Ring Around the Rosey
Pop Goes the Weasel
Take Me Out to the Ball Game
London Bridge
One, Two, Buckle My Shoe

For Preschoolers
The Hokey Pokey
Go In and Out the Window
Where o Where Has My Little Dog Gone?
Get on Board Little Children
Love Somebody

For Kindergarten
Polly Wolly Doodle
She'll Be Comin' Round the Mountain
I've Been to London
B-I-N-G –O
I'v Been Working on the Railroad

For Elementary – 1-3
Michael Row Your Boat Ashore
Home on the Range
Cockles and Mussels
This Land is Your Land
Purple People Eater

For Elementary – 4-6
Amazing Grace
Swing Low Sweet Chariot
Down in the Valley
Yellow Submarine
On top of Old Smokey

Spanish Language Songs
De Colores
Un Elefante
La Cucaracha
La Bamba
Guantanamera

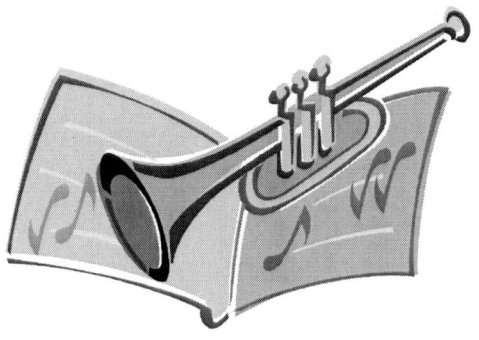

Chapter 8

TIME TO GET STARTED

Parents who are ready to get started with a personalized music program can proceed by doing the following:

- Check our songs for children list and begin by bringing music into your home. This list is only a beginning. The internet has many other children's song suggestions. Please check to be sure all songs are age appropriate.

- Depending on the age of your children, review the music programs in your area and start visiting them to find one which meets your budget and time.

- Check with the schools of your choice and decide if they meet your needs.

- Talk with other parents who have children in music programs; are they happy with the program they are in?

- If your school has a band program, talk to the program director and have your child give it a try.

    Whatever age level your children are at, use this guide and …
    ## **GET STARTED NOW !**

Chapter 9

INTERNET REFERENCES FOR CHIDREN'S LEARNING PROCESS

From Heartbeat to Steady Beat – Music and the Unborn Child
MENC: The National Association for Music Education | www.menc.org | 1806 Robert Fulton Drive| Reston, VA 20191 | 2011 MENCC

Time Invested in Practicing Pays Off For Young Musicians, Research Shows (A Harvard based study found that children who study a musical instrument for at least three years outperform children with no instrumental training.) Science Daily, Nov. 5, 2008

Music training helps improve certain memory capabilities outside of music. Musicians show improvement in auditory verbal memory and auditory attention.
www.psychologytoday.com/blog/memory-medic/2010/07

The Power of Music: the impact on the intellectual, social and personal development of children and young people. International Journal of Music Education | Aug. 1, 2010. p. 28 | 269-289.

Eco-Music for Kids – What better way to learn about the earth than to learn about the many ways you can care for the environment than to sing about them… www.leonardodicapprio.org/kids/music.html -

Kids Art and Music – Kids OLR | www.kidsolr.com/arts_music/index.html – Cached Chuckleberries.com—to create great age appropriate music for kids outgrowing Sesame Street and Barney.

My Name Music – Personalized music for kids |The music is set for children from newborn to age 8. www.mynamemusic.com/

Classical Music for Kids mp3s Download the full Classical Music for Kids, Aug. 2007   www.emusic.com

Kid songs: Children's Songs. Music CDs. DVDs Songs and Free Kid Songs www.kidsongs.com

Hebrew Music for Kids – By Matan Ariel songs in Hebrew arranged for Children and Toddlers. www.israel.com/booklist.asp?

How to read Piano Music for kids | ehow.com Learn to play the piano. www.ehow.com

Rockosaurus Rex - Metal & Rock Kids Music | www.rockosaurusrex.com/ - cached

The Music Room – Barbara Kerley – www.suzyred.com/music - cached Words and music you can sing every day.

Music and Kids | AtHomeDad.org – www.athomedad.org |forums |Ask a Dad | Parenting
Curious, what do other Dads listen to when the kids are in the car?

KidSites.com - Music Site for Kids | www.kidsites.com/sites-edu/music.htm - Cached
Resource of 6900 classical music files in MIDI format from 525 Composers. Play or create music.

Classical Music for Children | Download and Stream Classical Music
www.classicalonline.com/music/classical-music-for children.html –Cached

Super Simple Songs – Easy English songs for kids
www.supersimplesongs.com/ - cached. Super simple are designed for ESL teachers to sing with her students.

Children's Bible Songs – All round fun songs.
www.maynardsgroovytunes.co.uk/ - cached. Great new kid's bible songs. Get the lyrics, action and motion. Download
Mp3s and FREE also PDF Sheet Music.

Sound of Music Bios – with original movie cast.
www.angelacarwright.com/soundof.htm - Cached. The original, grown up, cast reviews the movie 45 years later.

Christmas songs and lyrics for kids.
www.allthingschristmas.com/northpole/songs.html - cached. Christmas Carol lyrics and music in MIDI format for you to listen to on your computer.

Kids Benefit from Music Instruction – Music Research Study April 7, 2008 Excerpt
From: www.makingmusicfun.net.

Music for Children – social and emotional learning – research. May 7, 2011.
www.drmacmusic.com/research-on-songs-and-activites-to-boost-children...cached

MUSICAL IS ALMOST MAGICAL as a medium to enhance children's social and emotional skills.
Research: Teaching Music to Children with Autism: Understandings…Dec. 7, 2009

www.autism.healingthresholds.com. Rehearsal routines and movements may be useful tools for music teachers who teach autistic children.

Welcome | MUSIC Together Princeton Lab. School.
www.musictogetherprincestoon.com
May 19, 2011. The Music Together curriculum was developed based on research about both how young children learn and about how they develop musically.

The Correlation between Music and Math: A NEUROBIOLOGY PERSPEDTUS
www.seerendip.brynmawr.edu/exchange/node/1869 - Cached, Jan. 16, 2008
Most research shows that when children are trained in music at a young age, they tend to improve in the math skills.

Research shows Music Learning improves Children's IQ Scores www.musiclearningforkids.com/educators-research- Cached

New research on music that boosts social and emotional skills
www.edutopia.org >-Groups>Art/Music Drama-cached
New study Music Education Helps Kids Brains with Sound Stimuli.

Chapter 10

RESEARCH REFERENCES

The following are selected research projects which were focused on the effect that music has on a child's learning process.

Aleman, A – Music training and mental imagery ability. Neuropsychology, 2000 –
The results suggest that music training may improve both musical and non-musical auditory imagery. Journal of Experimental Psychology Learning, memory and cognition.

Abrams, R. M (1995) Some Aspects of the Fetal Sound Environment. *Perception and cognition of music (pp 83-101). Philadelphia, PA ; Psychology Press.*

Autism, Education: Music Therapy and Language: Autism Research Institute
www.autism.com/edu_music_therapy.asp - Autism cached. Music Therapy is particularly useful with autistic children owing in part to the nonverbal nature of its structure.

Baby Music – About Music Classes at Kindermusik for babies.
www.kindermusik.com/abaout/ - cached

Behavioral Cognition Neuroscience Revue, Dec.1, 2005, 4: 235-261

Brain –
One year of musical training affects development of auditory cortical – evoked fields in young children – Oct. 1, 2006 – 2593 – 2604

Brothers, L, Shaw, GL, Wright, E. Duration of extended mental music rehearsals are remarkably reproducible in higher level human performances. Neurol Rs., 1993; 15: 413 – 416.

Cerebral Cortex, March 1, 2009, 19:" 712 -723. Music Training Influences Linguistic Abilities in 8 year olds. More Evidence for Brain Plasticity

Dannenberg, R. B. A machine learning approach to musical style recognition, 1997. www.Repository.cmu.edu – Machine learning has been shown to improve the performance of many per – caption and classification systems including speech recognition and vision systems.

Hetland, Lois, Learning to Make Music Enhances Special Reasoning. Journal of Aesthetic Education, Vol. 34, No.5, 3-4 Fall/Winter 2000 (c) 2000. Board of Trustees - University of Illinois Press.

Hurwitz, I – Nonmusical Effect of the Kodaly Music Curriculum in Primary Grade Children. Rhythmic elements as well as those of pitch and tone were fund to improve performance. Journal of Learning. 1975 –
www.idx.sagepub.com
Journal of Research in Music Education, July 1, 2011 | 59, 126 -145 – A Demographic
Profile of High School Music Ensemble Students in the United States.

Klemm, William, D.V.M., PhD. Music Training Helps Learning & Memory.
Memory Medic – July 31, 2010.

Language and Music –The Relationship between Musical Skills, Music Training, and Intonation Analysis Skills. Language and Speech - June 1, 2007 – 50: 177-225.

Leng, x, Coding of music structure and the Trion model of cortex. Music Perception. 1990; 8: 49-62.

Moreno, Sylvain, Carlos Marques –Musical Training Influences Linguistic Abilities in 8-Year-Old Children: More Evidence for Brain Plasticity. Oxford Journals: Vol. 19 Issue 3 Pp. 712-723.

Neurosci, J. Musical Training Shapes Structural Brain Development, March 11, 2009
29: 3019-3025
http://pss.sagepub.com//content/15/8/511.short

Neurosci, J. Broca's Area Supports Enhanced Visuospatial Cognition in Orchestral Musicians. April 4, 2007 27: 3799-3808
http://pss.sagpub.com//content/15/8/511.short

Orff, Carl, History of Orff Instruction. www.classics for kids/teachers; Orff 101

Orff, Carl, The Carl Orff Approach – Google in Orff Approach.
Orff, Carl, Also available through Amazon.

Petche, H. EEG coherence and musical thinking. Music Perception 1993:: 11: 117-151

Psychology of Music – The effects of musical training on verbal memory. July 1, 2008 36: 353-365

Psychology of Music – The effects of piano lessons on the vocabulary and verbal sequencing skill of primary grade students - July 1, 2009 37: 325-347

Sarnthein, J. Persistent patterns of brain activity: An EEG coherent study of the positive effect of music on spatial-temporal-reasoning. Neural Res. 1997: 19: in press

Schellenberg, Glenn - Music Lessons Enhance IQ. Department of Psychology, University of Toronto at

Mississauga, ON, Canada L5L 1C6; e-mail g.schellenberg@utoronto.ca.

Shelter, D.J. Prelude to a Musical Life: Prenatal music experiences- (1985)
Music Educators Journal. 1971, (7). 26 - 27.

Tchalkovsky Research: Sixteen Songs for Children. Op.54 (TH 104)
www.tchalkovsky-research.net

Training Effects Brain – First Evidence That Musical Training Affects Brain Development –
www.sciencedaily.com/releases/2006/09/060920093024
Sep. 20, 2006 (Whereas previous studies have shown older children had improved IQ scores, this study shows younger children had improved.)

Bibliography

Abramson, Robert, M. Rhythm Games Book I. New York: Music and Movement Press, 1973.

Bernstein, Leonard, The Joy of Music. New York: Simon and Schuster, 1959. The Infinite Variety of Music, New York: Simon and Schuster, 1962.

Burley, Allen, Madelyn. Listening: The Forgotten Skill, New York: John Wiley and Sons, 1982.

Campbell, Don G. Music and Miracles. Wheaton, Illinois. Theosophical Publishing House, 1990.
Mozart Effect,

Cars – Beggs, Barbara. Your baby Needs Music: A Music Sound Book for babies up to Two Years Old. New York: St. Martin's Press, 1978.

Copland, Aaron. Music and Imagination, Cambridge, Mass: Harvard University Press, 1952.

De Beer, Sara (ed.) Open Ears: Musical Adventures for a New Generation. Roslyn, New York: Ellipsis Kids, 1995.

Drapper, Maureen, McCarthy. The Nature of Music – Beauty, Sound and Healing. Riverhead Putnam Inc., New York: 2000.

Hopkins, Antony. Understanding Music: Oxford University Press, 1993.

Khan, Hazrat Inayat The Mysticism of Sound and Music. Boston and London.

Machover, Wilma and Uszler, Marienne. Sound Choices, Guiding Your Child's Musical Experience. Oxford University Press, 1996.

CARMEN R. DE ANGELIS – AUTHOR

The author is a retired teacher of 41 years. He has earned a B.A., M.Ed., and C.A.S. (Certificate of Administrative Supervision) in education. Married and he and his wife have just celebrated their 50th anniversary. They have 13 grandchildren and one great grandchild.

Both the author and his wife have created a 501 C3 charitable organization called Waiting Doesn't Hurt, and a subdivision, Youth Outreach. Youth Outreach has, as its goals, first, to collect used musical instruments and lend them to needy children, second, to act as music advocates. In light of the second goal, Youth Outreach has helped create a high school music program where a music program was nonexistent.

Again, as music advocates, the members of the Youth Outreach team have been instrumental in the creation of this guide book for parents," Music Magic".

It is the authors' hope that parents read this guide and encourage their children to study music. Throughout life a child will grow meeting many challenges. Some challenges will be met making choices between socially acceptable options and those which are not socially acceptable. There are many advantages to learning to play a musical instrument but none is more important than how a child spends his/her time.

It is our desire to have students playing a musical instrument rather than making a choice which will have them spending their time getting into trouble.